SURPRISING DESIGNS

FROM TRADITIONAL QUILT BLOCKS

CAROLE M. FURE

That Patchwork Place

An Imprint of
Martingale & Company

Credits

Editor-in-Chief
Kerry I. Smith

Technical Editors
Janet White
Ursula Reikes

*Design & Production
Manager*
Cheryl Stevenson

Cover Designer
Jim Gerlitz

Text Designer
Kay Green

Copy Editor
Liz McGehee

Proofreader
Laurel Strand

Illustrator
Laurel Strand

Design Assistant
Marijane E. Figg

Photographer
Brent Kane

Surprising Designs from
Traditional Quilt Blocks

Martingale & Company
PO Box 118
Bothell, WA 98041-0118
USA

Dedication
This book is dedicated to the creative spirit in each of us.

Acknowledgments

Who knows how many people influence us in our growth. I suspect most everyone with whom we have contact. I extend my thanks to them all and especially to those who directly influenced this project. My sincere thanks go to:

My mother, Clarice Weber, who taught me needle crafts and showed me how a garment could look very different with just a small change of fabric or trim;

The many quilt instructors, authors, and friends who, by sharing their skills and techniques, expanded my horizons in quilting;

Sissy Gubbe and the staff at Northern Pines Quilt Shop, who provided a place for me to share the joy of block-pattern play with other quilters;

Rosemary Rosen, who was the spark that ignited this book;

Sally Bair, Sissy Gubbe, Barb Lemire, Sylvia Schmit, Vicki Tollander, the Peacemakers Quilting Group, and Ursula Reikes, who, through their constructive comments, contributed immensely to the clarity and completeness of this book;

And a very special thanks to my family, who gives me time and space to do my own thing.

Library of Congress Cataloging-in-Publication Data

Fure, Carole.
    Surprising designs from traditional quilt blocks : use a single block to create countless quilts / Carole M. Fure.
        p. cm.
    ISBN 1-56477-155-5
    1. Patchwork—Patterns. 2. Quilting—Patterns. 3. Patchwork quilts. I. Title.
TT835.F87 1998
746.46'041—dc21   98-4670
                                                                                        CIP

Printed in Hong Kong
03 02 01 00 99 98   6 5 4 3 2

TABLE OF CONTENTS

INTRODUCTION

"Wow! Would you look at that," I said to myself in amazement as I completed another block for my secret pal. I had decided I would send her a block each month—the same block, the same fabrics—but I would vary the fabric placement each time I made the block. I was surprised to see how different they looked. I was having so much fun that, after completing her twelve blocks, I made another eighteen for myself and still had not exhausted the block's potential. It seemed the more I played with the fabric placement, the more block patterns I discovered.

One day, when my sister was visiting, I laid out blocks on the floor, eager to show her my amazing discovery. When I did, I was again surprised by the unique designs that appeared at the edges of the blocks where they joined each other. "This would make a great quilt," I said, as I pointed to one block connection, and then another and another. I could hardly contain my excitement.

In my sixteen years of quilting, I had never felt so energized. I completed one quilt and went right on to the next. The more I played, the more I discovered, the more I created. Eager to share this process with other quilters, I began teaching classes in our local quilt shop. Several years later, at the suggestion of one of my students, I began recording the process so that all quilters might have access to it. This unique process of play is described in detail in *Surprising Designs*.

As I discovered, the first step in learning to create is learning to play. Play leads to discovery, which in turn leads to creativity. In this book, you will learn a unique method of fabric play. You will arrange and rearrange fabrics within a single quilt block and discover more surprising designs than you ever expected. By combining these block patterns in specific ways, you will be amazed at how you can change the overall look of the quilt. This method of fabric play will unlock your creativity. You will discover the incredible number of designs hidden within a single block.

This book describes a step-by-step method for designing and creating quilts. Use it to plan a quilt from its beginning to its completion, or use it to plan a specific aspect of a quilt, such as the overall design, the central block patterns, or the border blocks.

Planning a Quilt identifies the elements to consider in determining your quilt size, such as mattress size, intended use, block setting, and borders. The directions guide you through the planning process, from determining your quilt size to diagramming the initial quilt plan.

Designing a Quilt describes five basic block patterns and four traditional quilt designs and how you may modify them to fit your plan. This section also provides suggestions for creating quilt designs to fit a bed.

Choosing a Quilt Block provides ten sample blocks and directions for constructing a design board.

Selecting Fabric gives you a guide for successful fabric selection and a simple formula for determining the amount of fabric required. The complicated math has been done for you. Figures are provided in easy-to-use charts.

Cutting provides guidelines for cutting your fabric and tips for creating a fabric palette.

Creating Block Patterns and Quilt Designs describes in detail a unique method for creating block patterns to fit your quilt design. As you use this method, you will experience firsthand the effect of fabric placement on block pattern and quilt design. Also included in this section are 110 block patterns and ten quilt mock-ups, which demonstrate the use of some of these patterns.

The Quilt Show contains examples of ten quilts I made using the process described in this book. Included for each is the initial quilt plan and design, a photograph of the finished quilt, and comments regarding the design process. I hope, in viewing them, you will realize that, with the aid of the play process described in this book, you, too, can discover and create surprising designs.

PLANNING A QUILT

When you begin to think of making a quilt, a flood of options comes rushing in: fabric, quilt size, pattern, color, blocks, yardage, borders. This deluge of choices can overwhelm you if you do not know where to begin.

Making a plan is the starting point of the quiltmaking process. A plan gives you a framework on which to hang your ideas and makes it easier to choose among the options possible for your quilt. The first issues in formulating the quilt plan are determining the desired size of the quilt and how you will achieve that size. Most of the quilts I make are bed size. Use the following steps to determine the size for a bed quilt. If the quilt you intend to make will hang on a wall, you do not need to consider the mattress size, drop, or pillow. The size of your quilt depends on the amount of space available on your wall.

The size of a bed quilt depends on the mattress size and intended use, so first, **select the appropriate mattress size.**

Standard Mattress Sizes

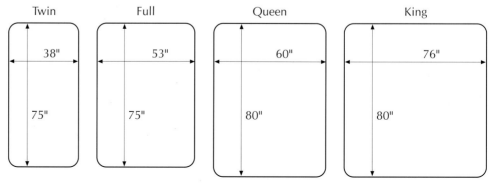

Long twin and long full are 80". California King is 72" x 84".

Water Bed Mattress Sizes

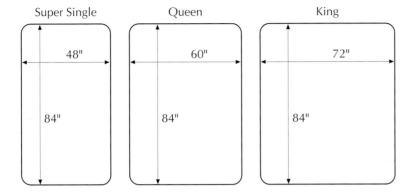

Next, **determine the intended use.** A quilt can be used as a blanket, a comforter (with or without dust ruffle), or a bedspread that reaches to the floor. Each use requires a different quilt size.

For a quilt to be used as a *blanket*, add 15″ to each side and to the length of the mattress. This will give the quilt sufficient size so all your body parts remain covered when you roll over in bed.

If the quilt is to be used as a *comforter*, add 15″ to each side and to the length of the mattress, then add an additional 15″ to the length for the pillow and pillow tuck.

If the quilt is to be used as a *bedspread* to reach the floor, add 20″ to each side and to the length of the mattress, then add an additional 15″ to the length for the pillow and pillow tuck. Mattresses, box springs, and bed frames vary somewhat in depth. Measure the distance from the mattress top to the floor (the drop) to ensure that your quilt will be the correct size.

Calculate the desired quilt size, using the chart below. The example is for a comforter-size quilt.

	FILL IN YOUR QUILT		EXAMPLE	
	Width	Length	Width	Length
Mattress Size			53″	75″
Quilt Drop: Sides			30″ (2 x 15″)	—
Quilt Drop: End			—	15″
Pillow Tuck			—	15″
Desired Quilt Size			83″	105″

The next step in planning your quilt is to determine *how* the quilt size will be achieved. This step involves selecting a block setting, determining the number of blocks, and deciding on the type of borders you will use to complete the design.

Choose your block setting. The blocks in a quilt are either set square, with block sides parallel to the sides of the quilt, or on point, with block sides at a 45° angle to the sides of the quilt. If you choose an on-point setting, continue on page 14.

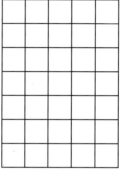

Square Set

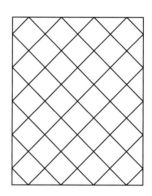

On-Point Set

Square Settings

All calculations in this book are based on a 12" finished block. If you plan to use a square setting, divide the desired quilt size, both the width and the length, by 12" to find the *approximate* number of blocks needed for the width and length of your quilt. If your block is of a different size, divide by that number.

| | Fill in Your Quilt | | Example | |
	Width	Length	Width	Length
Desired Quilt Size			83"	105"
Divide by Block Size			12"	12"
Number of Blocks (approx.)			6.9	8.75

The final steps in planning your quilt are to **determine the exact number of quilt blocks** you will need and whether or not you will use borders. You may complete your quilt plan by rounding the number of quilt blocks *up*.

	FILL IN YOUR QUILT		EXAMPLE	
	Width	Length	Width	Length
Desired Quilt Size			83"	105"
Number of Blocks			6.9	8.75
Round Up			7	9
Quilt Size (Blocks x 12")			84"	108"

Another option is to round the number of quilt blocks *down* and add an outer border.

	FILL IN YOUR QUILT		EXAMPLE	
	Width	Length	Width	Length
Desired Quilt Size			83"	105"
Number of Blocks			6.9	8.75
Round Down			6	8
Quilt Size (Blocks x 12")			72"	96"
5" Outer Border			10"	10"
Quilt Size with Borders			82"	106"

You may place borders *within* a quilt as well as around the edges. Inner borders can frame central designs and add size to a quilt. Inner borders must measure 6″ finished for the outer 12″ blocks to fit. (For blocks of other sizes to fit, the width of the inner borders must be one-half the finished block size.) Inner borders that do not reach the edge of the quilt are not included in calculating the quilt size.

Borders do not reach edge of quilt.   Borders reach edge of quilt.

	BORDER DOES NOT REACH EDGE	BORDER REACHES EDGE
Desired Quilt Size	83" x 105"	83" x 105"
Number of Blocks	7 x 9	6 x 8
6" Border	—	12" x 12"
Quilt Size	84" x 108"	84" x 108"

Quilt Plans Using a Square Setting

The following examples show quilt plans with a square setting. All figures are finished measurements.

SQUARE SET WITHOUT BORDERS

	Width	Length
Desired Size	83"	105
Blocks	7	9
Quilt Size	84"	108"

Square Set with Outer Border

	Width	Length
Desired Size	83"	105"
Blocks	6	8
Size	72"	96"
5" Border	10"	10"
Quilt Size	82"	106"

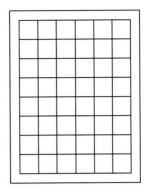

Square Set with Lattice and Outer Border

	Width	Length
Desired Size	83"	105"
Blocks	5	7
Size	60"	84"
2" Lattice	8"	12"
6" Border	12"	12"
Quilt Size	80"	108"

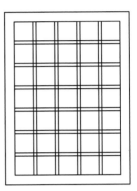

Square Set with Strippy Vertical Inner Borders and Outer Border

	Width	Length
Desired Size	83"	105"
Blocks	5	8
Size	60"	96"
4" Inner Border	16"	—
4" Outer Border	8"	8"
Quilt Size	84"	104"

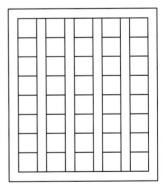

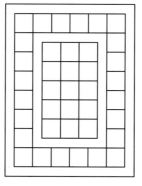

SQUARE SET WITH INNER AND OUTER BORDERS

	Width	Length
Desired Size	83"	105"
Blocks	6	8
Size	72"	96"
6" Inner Border	–	–
5" Outer Border	10"	10"
Quilt Size	82"	106"

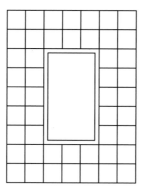

SQUARE SET WITH INNER BORDER

	Width	Length
Desired Size	83"	105"
Blocks	7	9
Size	84"	108"
Inner Space (36" x 36")*	–	–
Quilt Size	84"	108"

*Includes 3" border

Draw your quilt plan on the enclosed graph paper. Include borders and their measurements if they are part of your plan. Make ten copies and turn to page 21 to design your quilt top.

ON-POINT SETTINGS

If you are using an on-point setting in your design, you must use the diagonal measurement of a block or border as the width. In an on-point set, a 12″ finished block measures 17″ (rounded off) from corner to corner. A 6″ border placed on the diagonal measures 8.5″ across. See the table below for diagonal measurements of blocks from 1″ to 20″ square. The formula used to calculate diagonal measurements is located in the appendix on page 83.

WIDTH OF ON-POINT
BLOCKS AND BORDERS

Block or Border	Diagonal
1″	1.4″
2″	2.8″
3″	4.2″
4″	5.7″
5″	7″
6″	8.5″
7″	9.9″
8″	11.3″
9″	12.7″
10″	14.1″
11″	15.6″
12″	16.9″
13″	18.4″
14″	19.8″
15″	21.2″
16″	22.6″
17″	24″
18″	25.5″
19″	26.9″
20″	28.3″

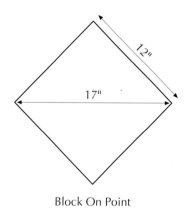

Block On Point

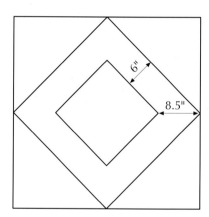

Border on Diagonal

To determine the *approximate* number of 12″ blocks needed for your quilt, divide the desired quilt size, both the width and the length, by 17″.

| | FILL IN YOUR QUILT | | EXAMPLE | |
	Width	Length	Width	Length
Desired Quilt Size			83″	105″
Divide by Diagonal			17″	17″
Number of Blocks			4.9	6.2

The final step in planning your quilt is to **determine the exact number of quilt blocks** you will need and whether or not you will use borders. You may complete your quilt plan by rounding *off* the number of quilt blocks needed.

| | FILL IN YOUR QUILT | | EXAMPLE | |
	Width	Length	Width	Length
Desired Quilt Size			83"	105"
Number of Blocks Needed			4.9	6.2
Round Off			5	6
Quilt Size (Blocks x 17")			85"	102"

Another option is to *decrease* the number of quilt blocks to accommodate an outer border.

| | FILL IN YOUR QUILT | | EXAMPLE | |
	Width	Length	Width	Length
Desired Quilt Size			83"	105"
Number of Blocks Needed			4.9	6.2
Decreased Number of Blocks			4	5
Quilt Size (Blocks x 17")			68"	85"
8" Outer Borders			16"	16"
Quilt Size with Borders			84"	101"

You may also place borders within a quilt in an on-point setting. Plan them the same way as for straight settings. Inner borders must measure 6″ in width (finished) for the outer 12″ blocks to fit. (For blocks of other sizes to fit, the inner borders must be one-half the finished block size.) Inner borders that do not reach the edge of the quilt are not included in calculating the quilt size.

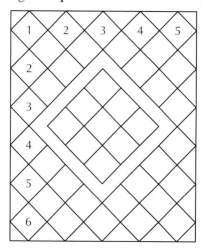

Border does not reach edge of quilt.

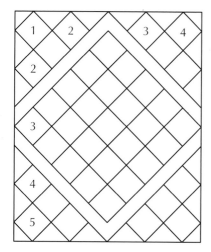

Border reaches edge of quilt.

	BORDER DOES NOT REACH EDGE	BORDER REACHES EDGE
Desired Quilt Size	83″ x 105″	83″ x 105″
Number of Blocks	5 x 6	4 x 5
6″ Border	–	17″ x 17″ (8.5″ x 2)
Quilt Size	85″ x 102″	85″ x 102″

When placing inner borders on the diagonal in a square setting or straight in an on-point setting, use a border one-half the diagonal measurement of the finished block. The inner borders must measure 8.5" finished (½ of 17") for the outer 12" blocks to fit. Refer to the chart on page 14.

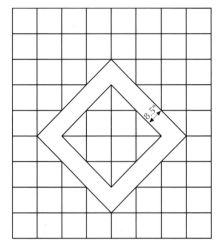

Square Set with Diagonal Inner Border

On-Point Set with Square Inner Border

Quilt Plans Using an On-Point Setting

The following examples show quilt plans with an on-point setting. All figures are finished measurements.

ON-POINT SET WITHOUT BORDER

	Width	Length
Desired Size	83"	105"
Blocks	5	6
Quilt Size	85"	102"

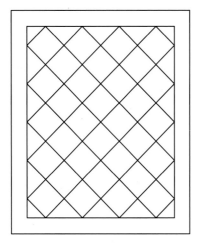

On-Point Set with Outer Border

	Width	Length
Desired Size	83"	105"
Blocks	4	5
Size	68"	85"
8" Border	16"	16"
Quilt Size	84"	101"

On-Point Set with Lattice and Outer Border

	Width	Length
Desired Size	83"	105"
Blocks	4	5
Size	68"	85"
2" Lattice	11.2"	14"
	(2.8" x 4)	(2.8" x 5)
3" Border	6"	6"
Quilt Size	85"	105"

On-Point Set with Vertical Inner Borders and Outer Border

	Width	Length
Desired Size	83"	105"
Blocks	4	6
Size	68"	102"
3" Inner Border	9"	—
3" Outer Border	6"	6"
Quilt Size	83"	108"

On-Point Set with Inner Border

	Width	Length
Desired Size	83"	105"
Blocks	5	6
Size	85"	102"
6" Inner Border	–	–
Quilt Size	85"	102"

On-Point Set with Inner Border

	Width	Length
Desired Size	83"	105"
Blocks	4	5
Size	68"	85"
6" Border* (8.5" x 2)	17"	17"
Quilt Size	85"	102"

*This border reaches the edge of the quilt.

Draw your quilt plan on the enclosed graph paper. Include borders and their measurements if they are part of your plan. Make ten copies and turn to the next section to design your quilt top.

DESIGNING A QUILT

I'm sure you have noticed how some quilts attract you like a magnet, while others seem to leave you limp. You may have asked yourself why. What draws us to one and not the other? The experts tell us it is color and design. It is not just one or the other, but the relationship between these two elements that determines the success of a quilt. The information that follows will help you understand this relationship.

Before beginning to design, let's define a few terms. I refer to the *quilt design* as the overall look of the quilt surface, and *block pattern* as the look of the individual quilt block. You can create different block patterns by rearranging the fabrics within a single quilt block. Combining these block patterns in specific ways determines the surface design and overall look of your quilt.

Example: Block pattern + Block pattern = Quilt design

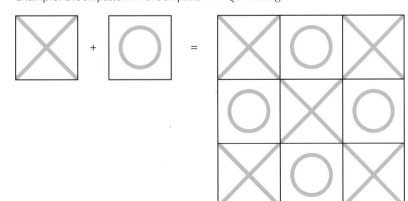

The following symbols have been used to represent some basic block patterns.

This symbol represents a *center* block pattern. This block pattern can stand alone. It does not need another block pattern to complete its design. Examples of center block patterns are stars, baskets, and pinwheels.

The *X* block is a pattern that runs diagonally from corner to corner. Alternate it with another block and it creates grid lines across the quilt surface. Make an X block pattern by placing your dark fabrics in lines that cross the block from corner to corner.

The *cross* block pattern runs across the block from side to side and from top to bottom. When alternated with another block pattern, it also creates a grid design across the quilt. To create a cross block pattern, place your dark fabric in lines across the block horizontally and vertically.

The *strippy* block pattern, when placed in rows, creates a line design running in one direction only (for example, up and down). Use this block pattern for borders and in medallion quilt designs as well as in strippy quilt designs. To create a strippy block pattern, place dark fabric in a line from the top of the block to the bottom.

This symbol represents a *repeat* block pattern that creates a secondary pattern at the edges of the block where it joins the next block. It is a more challenging pattern to work with because the secondary design is not obvious until blocks are joined together. To create a repeat block pattern, place some of your dark fabric at the edges of the block.

In this section, we will focus on the element of *quilt design*, that is, the overall look of the quilt surface. There are three aspects to consider when designing your quilt surface: the basic quilt design, the borders, and the bed surface areas.

Basic Quilt Designs

There are four basic, traditional quilt designs. By varying and combining these designs, you can create unique and interesting quilt tops. The four basic quilt designs are repeat block, alternate block, strippy, and medallion.

In the *repeat block* design, a single block pattern repeats to form the overall quilt design.

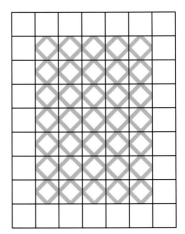 

Single Block Pattern

Repeat Block Pattern (Square Set)   Repeat Block Pattern (On-Point Set)

In the *alternate block* design, two block patterns alternate, like a checkerboard. The connections at the block corners and/or block sides create secondary patterns. Alternate block designs, in square sets, require an odd number of blocks across and down for balance.

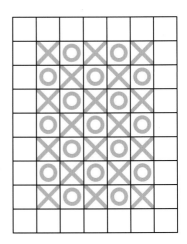 

Two-Block Patterns

Alternate Block (Square Set)   Alternate Block (On-Point Set)

In the *strippy* design, blocks form rows across the quilt top. These rows may run across the quilt from side to side, up and down, or diagonally.

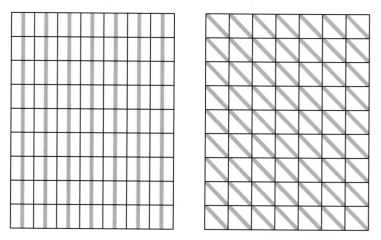

Strippy Design (Square Set)

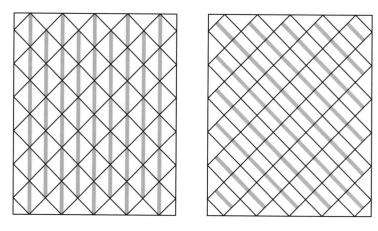

Strippy Design (On-Point Set)

In the *medallion* design, blocks and/or borders form frames around a central block or blocks. The frames may be square, diamond-shaped, or a combination of the two.

Four-Block Center   One-Block Center

Medallion Design (Square Set)

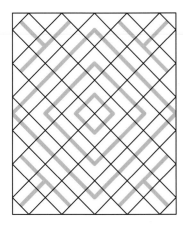
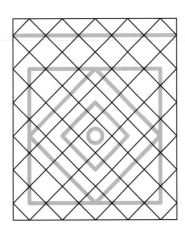

Four-Block Center   One-Block Center

Medallion Design (On-Point Set)

BORDERS

Borders add another design element to your quilt. Most borders are strips of cloth added to the outer edges. Another possibility is to use the same block as in the center of the quilt, but modify the patterns of the outer row of blocks (by changing the placement of the fabrics) to form a frame for the central design. You can also design narrow inner borders using half blocks.

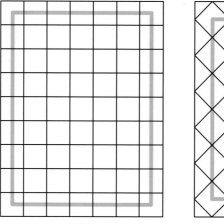

Border (Square Set)   Border (On-Point Set)

BED SURFACE AREAS

There are three areas of the bed to consider: the part of the quilt that covers the pillow, the side and end drops, and the top surface of the bed. The pillow cover is the top 18" of the quilt. The side and end drops are the parts of the quilt that hang from the top edge of the bed to the floor. The top surface of the bed is the remaining quilt top, minus approximately 8" to 12", which is tucked under the pillow. Keep the bed surface areas in mind while planning your quilt design to enhance the beauty of the quilt when placed on the bed, and to prevent the design from getting cut off by the pillow tuck or running over the edge of the bed.

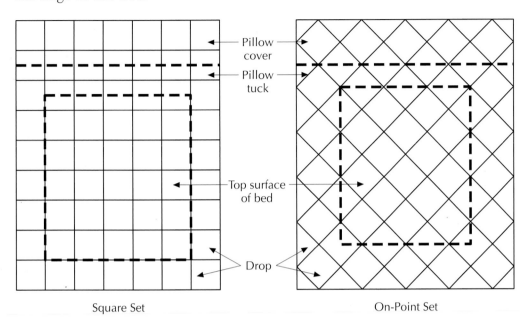

Pillow cover
Pillow tuck
Top surface of bed
Drop

Square Set   On-Point Set

You may want to place different designs across the pillow cover, around the drop, and on the top surface of the bed. You can also separate the top-surface design area from the drop with an inner border.

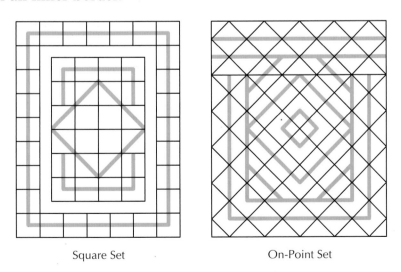

Square Set   On-Point Set

Using a colored pen, draw your quilt design onto a copy of the quilt plan you drew in the last section. Experiment on the copies to determine which design best suits your needs. Once you've chosen your favorite design, you are ready to choose a quilt block.

Choosing a Quilt Block

The quilt block is the cornerstone of your quilt. It determines the number and quality of the block patterns and, ultimately, the quilt design. As you select your quilt block, consider the number of pieces in the block. The number of pieces determines the choices you have for fabric placement and, consequently, the options you have for creating block patterns. I like to work with blocks containing from fifty to seventy pieces. Blocks with fewer pieces will work, but your options for block patterns will be limited.

Another consideration in selecting a block is the ease and accuracy with which you can cut the pieces. Creating block patterns is fun. You don't want to lose the fun struggling to cut difficult pieces.

It is not necessary to choose more than a single block to carry out your quilt design. A single block can provide many patterns to work with. Ten blocks are shown on pages 29–31, but don't limit yourself to these. Select your block from any source available to you. If you keep in mind the number of pieces and ease of cutting as you select your block, your choice will provide interesting design options and pleasure in the process.

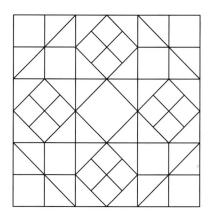

Aunt Vinah's Favorite

61 pieces
Seam allowances are included.

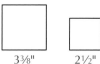

3⅜"   2½"   2⅞"   2"

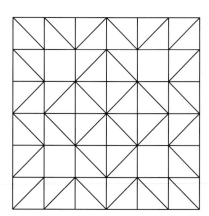

Hopscotch

68 pieces
Seam allowances are included.

2½"   2⅞"

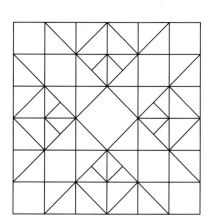

Christmas Star

69 pieces
Seam allowances are included.

3⅜"   2½"   2⅞"   2⅜"

All Hallows

72 pieces
Seam allowances are included.

2⅞"

Capital T

60 pieces
Seam allowances are included.

2½"   2⅞"

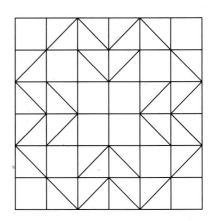

Wyoming Valley

65 pieces
Seam allowances are included.

3⅜"   2½"   2⅞"

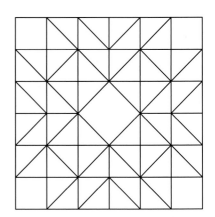

Combination Star

69 pieces
Seam allowances are included.

3⅜"   2⅞"

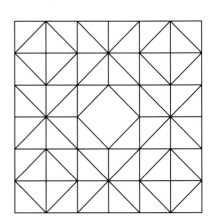

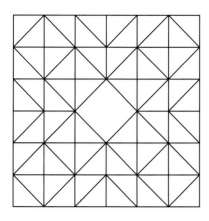

Swing in the Center

69 pieces
Seam allowances are included.

3⅜"   2⅞"

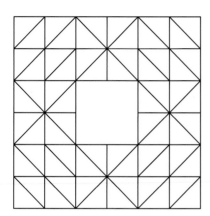

Jackknife

65 pieces
Seam allowances are included.

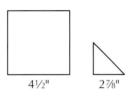

4½"   2⅞"

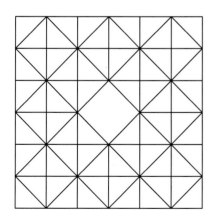

Courthouse Square

69 pieces
Seam allowances are included.

3⅜"   2⅞"

Block Design Board

Your next step is to make a design board if you don't already have one. You will find this tool essential in discovering the pattern potential of the block you have selected.

To make a block design board, you will need the following: 20" square of paper; pencil; ruler; drafting square; eraser; fine-point black marker; tape; 20" square of muslin; permanent, fine-point black fabric marker; and 20" square of hardboard.

The finished size of all the blocks used in planning the quilt designs in this book is 12". The block on your design board will be larger to accommodate the seam allowances of your fabric pieces.

1. Using a pencil, draw a 15" square on a piece of paper. If you planned your quilt using a different-size block, add 2" to 3" to the finished size of the block.
2. Draft your chosen block to fit the 15" square. For example, if you selected a block from this book, divide the square into 6 sections by drawing 5 lines each way. Subdivide these sections, drawing in the lines of your chosen block.
3. Erase any pencil lines that are strictly drafting lines, leaving only your block-piecing lines.
4. Darken these remaining lines with a fine-point black marker.
5. Tape the paper drawing to your work surface.
6. Center a 20" x 20" piece of white muslin over the paper drawing and tape it down.
7. Using a ruler, trace the paper drawing onto the white muslin with a permanent, fine-point black fabric marker.
8. Remove the muslin drawing of your block from your work surface and secure with tape to the hardboard. This is your design board.

Think of the design board as your canvas. You will use it throughout the creation of your quilt: as a guide for fabric placement, as a tool for viewing your new block pattern, and as a carrier for transporting your block pattern to your sewing machine and ironing board.

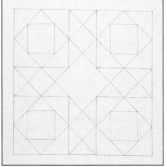

Joseph's Coat

SELECTING FABRIC

Three ingredients are necessary for successful fabric selection: personal preference, contrast, and spark. Personal preference usually plays the largest role in fabric and color choices. My sister may go berserk over a fabric that would put me to sleep, and vice versa. Contrast, the relationship of light against dark, is what makes the design of the quilt appear. Without it, no pattern would leap to your eye. You would not see the Churn Dash or the Feathered Star you painstakingly pieced. "Spark" is my word for the bright color that gives life and energy to the quilt. It determines whether a quilt is shy and retiring or confident and refreshing.

Here is an easy process for successful fabric selection. As you make your choices, keep in mind this one caution: fabrics with an obvious directional print do not work well because you will not be able to control the direction of the print.

First, choose a multicolor fabric that you like. Use a fabric in the medium value range (that is, not too dark and not too light). This fabric is called your focus fabric. You will follow the color scheme of your focus fabric to select the other fabrics for your quilt, so that the color scheme for the entire quilt will be as pleasing to you as your first fabric choice.

Second, using the focus fabric as a guide, choose a very dark coordinating fabric. This dark fabric will most likely determine the overall color of your quilt. If you want a predominantly blue quilt, choose a dark blue fabric. (Keep in mind also, that if you are using whole-cloth borders, the color of the outer border tends to determine the color of the quilt.)

Third, using the focus fabric as a guide, choose a very light fabric. This is your background fabric.

Fourth, using the focus fabric as a guide, choose a medium fabric.

Fifth, using the focus fabric as a guide, choose a bright, accent fabric. You may resist this fifth step. Bright fabric can be a bit overwhelming, especially when you are looking at a whole bolt. You will use only small amounts of this fabric. These sprinklings of bright color scattered across your quilt will make it sparkle.

Magic Yardage Formula

I have always kept track of the amount of fabric I use in each quilt that I make. Rather compulsive, I admit, but it has paid off. When I divided the surface area of the quilt by the amount of fabric I used, I came up with a Magic Number: 500. By reversing the process, I found that I could determine the amount of fabric I would need to make any quilt of any size!

Here is the magic formula: multiply the width of your quilt (in inches) by the length of your quilt, then divide by 500 to get the total yardage needed for your quilt.

Examples for Standard Bed-Size Quilts

	Width	x	Length	=	Surface Area	÷	Divide by	=	Total Yards
Twin	68"	x	90"	=	6,120	÷	500	=	12¼
Full	83"	x	90"	=	7,470	÷	500	=	15
Queen	90"	x	95"	=	8,550	÷	500	=	17
King	106"	x	95"	=	10,070	÷	500	=	20

I allot one-half the total yardage for the light background fabric and divide the remaining half among the other four fabrics, giving a little less to the bright accent fabric. If you are using whole-cloth borders, you may want to allot more yardage to that color.

For example, a full-size quilt, 83" x 90", requires 15 total yards of fabric. I divide the total amount as follows:

7½ yards of light background fabric
2 yards of focus fabric
2 yards of dark fabric
2 yards of medium fabric
1½ yards of accent fabric

FABRIC RECORDS

I recommend that you keep records of the fabric amounts you use in making each of your quilts. With the information you gather, you can modify the Magic Number to fit your specific style. You can adjust the total yardage purchased and/ or make changes in the way you allot the fabric. If you find you always need less fabric and don't want any left over for your stash (a preference not common among quilters), you can increase the Magic Number to 600 or 700. If you find that you typically run short of fabric and don't have a good friend with an adequate supply, you can decrease the Magic Number to 400. Create a chart like the one below and use it to record the amount of fabric purchased, the amount used, and the fabric remaining as you make your quilts.

Quilt Name: _____ Quilt Size: _____

Color	Yards Purchased	Yards Used	Yards Remaining
_____	_____	_____	_____
_____	_____	_____	_____
_____	_____	_____	_____
_____	_____	_____	_____
_____	_____	_____	_____
_____	_____	_____	_____
_____	_____	_____	_____
_____	_____	_____	_____
_____	_____	_____	_____

CUTTING

When I cut fabric for a quilt, I like to cut the larger quilt pieces first, then the smaller ones. I cut whole-cloth borders along the length of the fabric, because there is the least stretch along the lengthwise grain. Quilt designs using an on-point set require special side and corner *setting* triangles. I cut whole-cloth borders and setting triangles before I cut block pieces. If I change my mind later about using a whole-cloth border, I can cut it into block pieces, but I cannot do the reverse.

Like a painter who has a palette of paints to play with, you need a palette of block pieces to play with as you create your block pattern. To develop your palette, cut each block piece from each of your five fabrics. If the block has three different pieces, you will have fifteen stacks of cut pieces, one stack for each block piece in each fabric. Cut a few more and begin with approximately twenty-five pieces in each stack. For those blocks which have a large center square, cut only one or two pieces from each fabric. This is your fabric palette.

Block pieces included in this book are shown *with* seam allowances. For the triangles, cut a square in half diagonally. For example, a 2⅞" square cut in half diagonally will give you two 2⅞" triangles.

SETTING TRIANGLES FOR ON-POINT SETTINGS

For quilt designs using an on-point setting, squares cut diagonally provide the special side and corner setting triangles that fill in the edges and ensure that the outside edges of the quilt are on the straight of grain. The size of the squares from which these triangles are cut depends upon the size of the block used in the quilt.

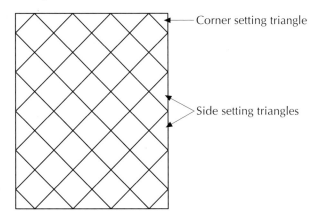

Corner setting triangle

Side setting triangles

For corner setting triangles in a quilt made of 12" finished blocks, cut 2 squares, each 9½" x 9½", then cut each square in half once diagonally to yield 4 corner setting triangles.

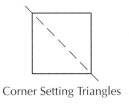

Corner Setting Triangles

To make side setting triangles for a quilt made of 12" finished blocks, cut a square 18½" x 18½", then cut the square in half twice diagonally. This will yield 4 side setting triangles. The number of side setting triangles required depends upon the size of your quilt.

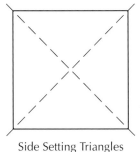

Side Setting Triangles

Use the following charts to determine the size of the squares to cut for corner and side setting triangles. The formulas used to calculate the size squares for these triangles are located in the appendix on pages 84–85.

For corner setting triangles, find the size of your quilt block, cut squares the size indicated, then cut them in half once diagonally. For side setting triangles, cut a square the indicated size, then cut it in half twice diagonally. Note that I have calculated these cut squares so that the triangles cut from them will be slightly larger than necessary. Trim the excess from the outside edges after the quilt top is sewn together.

CORNER SETTING TRIANGLES		SIDE SETTING TRIANGLES	
Quilt Block	Cut Square	Quilt Block	Cut Square
4"	4"	4"	7¼"
5"	4¾"	5"	8⅝"
6"	5¼"	6"	10"
7"	6"	7"	11½"
8"	6¾"	8"	12⅞"
9"	7½"	9"	14¼"
10"	8¼"	10"	15¾"
11"	8¾"	11"	17¼"
12"	9½"	12"	18½"
13"	10½"	13"	20"
14"	11"	14"	21⅜"
15"	11¾"	15"	22¾"
16"	12½"	16"	24¼"
17"	13¼"	17"	25⅝"
18"	13¾"	18"	27"
19"	14¾"	19"	28⅜"

CREATING BLOCK PATTERNS AND QUILT DESIGNS

The preparation phase is complete. You have planned your quilt, marked the quilt design on your plan, chosen a quilt block, and selected and cut the fabric. Now you are ready to play with block patterns on your design board.

By arranging the fabric pieces in specific ways within the quilt block, you can create block patterns which, when combined with other block patterns, will create the design you planned for your quilt surface. Remember, contrast is the key to design.

Following are several examples illustrating how the contrast of dark fabric against light fabric creates pattern, using the Joseph's Coat block. See how different block patterns appear in the same block when you alter the placement of the dark and light fabrics.

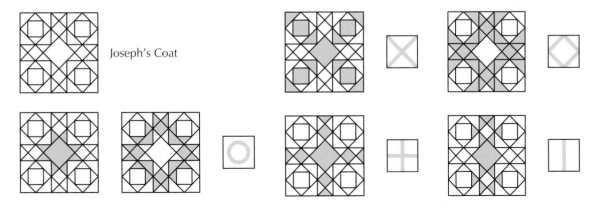

Joseph's Coat

You control the block pattern by choosing where you place your dark fabric. The dark fabric determines the *primary* pattern within the block, while the focus fabric and medium fabric determine the *secondary* pattern. Let me show you by using an example.

Example: Quilt plan 84" x 108"
(7 blocks x 9 blocks) square set,
Alternate Block quilt design
with outer row of blocks to form border.

1. Select one block from your quilt-design plan. This is the block pattern you will create on your design board.

Center Block Pattern

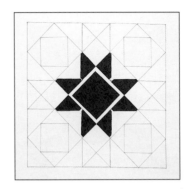

2. Place the dark fabric in the block on your design board in the same configuration as the green line in your block design plan. In a center block pattern, the green line stays within the block. Placing the dark fabric in the middle keeps the pattern in the center of the block. Try replacing some of the dark fabric with accent fabric. This can give a little sparkle to the design and lighten up the heavy feeling of the dark pieces. This is the primary block pattern. Be sure you are satisfied that the primary block pattern achieves the task of the chosen block design; in this example, it should focus attention in the center of the block.

3. Place the focus and medium fabrics on your design board around the dark fabric in a pleasing arrangement. This creates the secondary block pattern. The secondary block pattern should support the primary block pattern, not compete with it. Repeating the secondary block pattern throughout the quilt creates a sense of unity in the design.

4. To complete your block pattern, add the light fabric around the outer edges of the block.

5. Take a look at the block and rearrange pieces if necessary. When you are satisfied that the primary block pattern has been achieved and the secondary block pattern is pleasing to you, sew the block together.

Now, design the second block in your two-block quilt plan.

X Block Pattern

1. Place the dark fabric on your design board in the same configuration as the green line in your second block design. In the **X** block pattern, the green line goes diagonally across the block from corner to corner. Place the dark fabric across the block from corner to corner as shown in the block drawing. This is the primary block pattern.

2. Place the focus fabric and medium fabric around the dark fabric on your design board in a pleasing manner. Now try replacing some of your fabric pieces with accent fabric to give your block pattern a little spark. This is the secondary block pattern. Does the secondary pattern support the primary pattern? If you can still see the **X** pattern in the secondary pattern, you will know that it supports the primary pattern.

3. Complete the block by placing the light fabric in the remaining outer positions.

4. When you are satisfied with both the primary and secondary block patterns, sew the block together.

Note: In a two-block quilt, one entire block may be the primary block pattern, while the other creates the secondary block pattern. In the two-block quilt example, you may want the stars to be the primary block pattern, and the grid created by the **X** block to be the secondary pattern. If this is your plan, use more of the dark and accent fabrics in the star block and less of the medium and focus fabrics. In the **X** block, use less of the dark and accent fabrics and more of the focus and medium fabrics. The strong dark and accent fabrics will draw your attention to the star block, making it the primary quilt pattern.

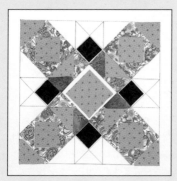

The function of a border is to end the design gracefully and to push the viewer's attention back into the center of the quilt. Sometimes the design, or parts of it, must extend into the border to avoid looking chopped off.

Lay your completed quilt blocks out on the floor or hang them on a design wall if you are fortunate enough to have one. Placing the blocks together as they will appear in the quilt will help you to see where the design should extend into the border.

Continue the primary block pattern to the *center* of the border blocks only, *not* to the outer edges. The outer portions of the border blocks contain and frame the design.

In the example below, the primary pattern of the **X** block crisscrossing the quilt looks unfinished unless it is carried into the center of the border (border block pattern #1). Stopping the **X** pattern at the center of the border block completes the quilt design and allows the line of dark pieces running up and down through the border blocks to frame and complete the border design.

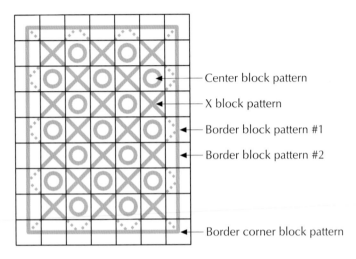

— Center block pattern

— X block pattern

— Border block pattern #1

— Border block pattern #2

— Border corner block pattern

The border requires two different side border blocks and a corner block. To create these blocks, use the same block pattern and the same process as for the main block patterns.

1. Place pieces of the dark fabric in the same positions as the green lines in your block design plan for the border blocks. In border block pattern #1, place dark pieces on the center line from top to bottom, then to continue the **X** pattern from the body of the quilt, place dark pieces from each inside corner to the center of the border block. In border block pattern #2, create a line of dark pieces from center top to bottom. In the corner block, place the dark pieces so that they turn the corner and so that they continue the **X** pattern into the center of the corner block.

Side-Border
Block Pattern #1

Side-Border
Block Pattern #2

Corner-Block
Border Pattern

2. Place the focus and medium fabrics around the dark fabric to create the secondary block pattern.

3. Complete your block pattern by placing the light fabric away from the dark fabric.

The individual block patterns may look peculiar, but when the blocks are sewn together, they create the overall design of the quilt.

THE QUILT SHOW

Quilters love quilt shows. At first, we love the pure sensual pleasure of viewing color and design, but then we begin selecting those quilts we like most. We want to know how the quilt was conceived, pulled off, and put together. Out comes the camera for a photograph and a napkin to draw on. I have a folder full of napkins and a shoe box full of photos.

In this section, you can sit back in the comfort of your home for a private showing of ten quilts that were made using the process described in this book. *All the quilts were made using the same quilt block, Joseph's Coat.* The point is not that all quilts must be made using the same block, but that within a single block, there are enough patterns to create many unique and surprising quilt designs.

Which design do you like best? What would you do differently? Study the quilt-design plan to see how it corresponds with the quilt. No need for a napkin, it's all there for you. Included for each quilt are the initial quilt plan, a photograph of the finished quilt, and comments regarding the process. I hope that in viewing them, you will see the process at work and will realize that you, too, have the ability to unlock the surprising designs hidden in ordinary quilt blocks.

STRAWBERRY SHORTCAKE

*T*he blocks in this "sampler," set on point, are all the same, and the same five fabrics appear in each block. Different block patterns resulted when I varied the value placement within the blocks. I created the pieced border by arranging leftover pieces in a pleasing manner. To get the pieced border to fit the quilt, I adjusted the seam allowances. I used the dark green fabric rather than the light background fabric for the lattice, setting triangles, and outside border. Using the dark lattice next to the light background of the blocks makes each block (rather than the block pattern) stand out.

BY CAROLE M. FURE, 1991, DANBURY, WISCONSIN, 83" x 103". MACHINE QUILTED BY KAREN DEVRIES.

RASPBERRY PATCH

I used the same block in a square setting throughout this quilt. All five fabrics appear in each block, but I changed their placement to create different block patterns. Playing with fabric in crazy ways, knowing you don't have to sew the pieces together, helps to open the door to new ideas. Before sewing the blocks together, I placed them next to each other without lattice to see what secondary designs might occur at the edges of the block. A pieced half block repeats in the border. The corners are pieced quarter blocks.

BY CAROLE M. FURE, 1994,
DANBURY, WISCONSIN,
76" X 90".
MACHINE QUILTED BY
KAREN DEVRIES.

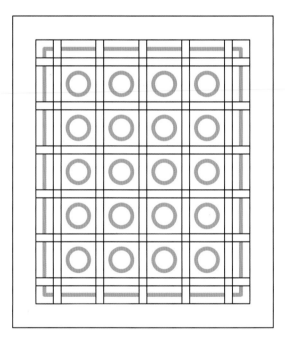

DESERT STAR

*T*his design began with a single block set on point surrounded by border-block patterns that form a central medallion. Simpler border-block patterns form rows around the medallion. The plain inner border reaches the edge of the quilt in one direction but not in the other. The design in the outer corners occurs when blocks connect with the adjacent blocks at their sides and corners. Although multiple block connections are challenging, they create more pleasing quilt designs. The focus fabric in this quilt was a tie-dyed print that blended well with the other fabrics.

By Carole M. Fure, 1992, Danbury, Wisconsin, 85" x 102". Machine quilted by Karen DeVries.

STAR MEDLEY

*T*his square-set quilt design alternates a star block pattern with an X pattern. The X block patterns (medium gold) join at their corners, forming a grid around the darker and brighter star block pattern. In this quilt, not all five fabrics were used in all blocks. The light, medium, focus, and small amounts of dark were used in the X block for less contrast, making the design less dominant. I used the light, dark, accent, and focus fabrics in the star block to create high contrast, making the design more prominent. I used lots of different accent fabrics in the star blocks and discovered that I liked the effect. I modified the X block pattern to create a border that brings the viewer's attention back into the quilt.

BY CAROLE M. FURE, 1992, DANBURY, WISCONSIN, 84" x 108". MACHINE QUILTED BY KAREN DEVRIES.

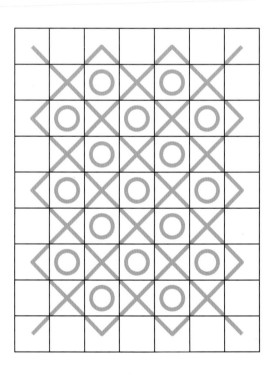

MYSTERY AND MISSION

A star pattern and a cross pattern alternate in this square-set quilt. The star pattern joins the cross pattern at its sides, creating a grid design. The colored background fabric decreases the intensity of contrast between light and dark, creating a muted overall design. Using multiple accent fabrics in the alternate blocks breaks the monotony of a one-color quilt. I modified the cross pattern to create the border.

By Carole M. Fure, 1995, Danbury, Wisconsin, 84" x 108". Machine quilted by Karen DeVries.

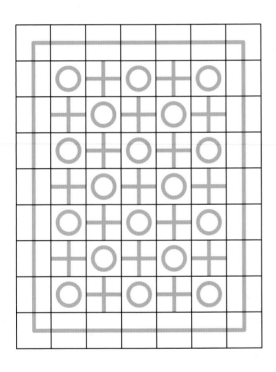

A GIFT

*T*he theme for this square-set strippy quilt is "the gift." The background of white and light-colored stars is the wrapping paper, and the dark strippy design is the ribbon. I experimented with color shading in this quilt. Although I used multiple fabrics, I applied the usual principle of using light, dark, medium, and accent fabrics. I kept all the color in the center of the blocks from top to bottom. The block patterns join each other at the top and bottom to carry the design up and down the quilt. A Rosette block pattern ends each row. At the corners of the blocks where they join each other, a star pattern of the light focus fabric formed. I finished off the edge of the quilt by using a portion of the block pattern to complete the background stars.

BY CAROLE M. FURE, 1993, DANBURY, WISCONSIN, 55" x 67". MACHINE QUILTED BY KAREN DEVRIES.

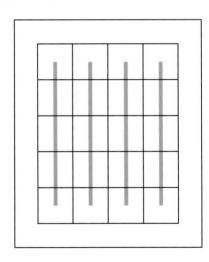

LISSA'S POOL

*T*his square-set asymmetrical block pattern looks like fish. In the original plan, the blocks were to be arranged in a traditional strippy design. I used a medium fabric against a light green background to create a strippy pattern of bubbles, while the dark, focus, and accent fabrics formed the fish. In using a medium fabric for the bubbles, the strippy design became the secondary pattern while the fish with their dark and bright fabrics became a primary center pattern. After I completed the blocks, the fish looked better offset. Shifting every other row made the fish look more natural, as if they were swimming. Offsetting the blocks further decreased the effectiveness of the secondary strippy design. The final quilt design plan is really a center block design rather than a strippy design. This quilt shows that plans are just that: "plans," subject to change.

By Carole M. Fure, 1994, Danbury, Wisconsin, 56" x 72". Machine quilted by Karen DeVries.

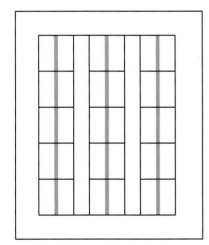

Original Plan

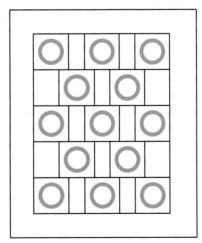

Final Plan

ROYAL SPLENDOR

I created the four-block center of this square-set medallion quilt by rotating a diagonal block pattern. Diagonal block patterns form the diamond surrounding the center medallion. The blocks at the centers of the top, bottom, and sides in the quilt plan belong to both the diamond design and the border design. I could not get the block pattern to carry out both design plans. I suppose the dark fabric could not serve two masters. It had to be loyal to either the diamond design or the border.

To solve a background fabric shortage, I used multiple shades of yellow, starting with light yellow in the center and gradually getting darker as I worked toward the edges of the quilt. The lighter background fabric in the center of the quilt creates a greater contrast with the dark, making the center design stronger. The darker background fabric around the edges of the quilt decreases the design contrast, bringing the viewer's attention back to the center.

By Carole M. Fure, 1995, Danbury, Wisconsin, 96" x 96". Machine quilted by Karen DeVries.

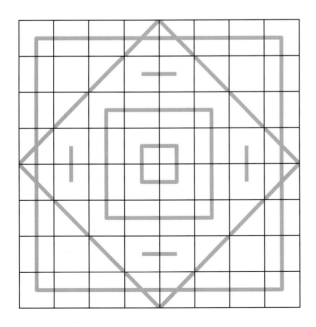

TWILIGHT STARS

*T*he star design of this repeat-block, scrappy quilt occurs where the blocks join at their sides. Placing the lighter blocks of this square-set quilt at the center and the darker ones at the edge of the quilt creates a more interesting overall design. The quilt is framed by three borders: a whole-cloth border, a pieced border, and another whole-cloth border. The pieced border design is the same as the diagonal pattern that criss-crosses the quilt.

BY CAROLE M. FURE, 1996, DANBURY, WISCONSIN, 90" X 114". MACHINE QUILTED BY KAREN DEVRIES.

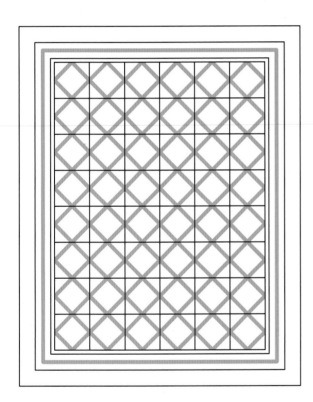

MARDI GRAS

*T*his square-set scrap quilt was made with the leftover pieces from my previous Joseph's Coat quilts. The interlocking rings form at the sides of the blocks by following through with a specific color from block to block. Modifying the block pattern and using a variegated color scheme creates a frame for the quilt. Large areas of tan background called for a subtle secondary design of white stars.

By Carole M. Fure, 1996, Danbury, Wisconsin, 79" x 103". Machine quilted by Karen DeVries.

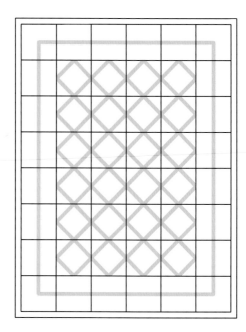

GALLERY OF BLOCK PATTERNS

To help you get started, eleven block patterns are shown for each of the ten blocks in this book. These block patterns are not exhaustive. I hope they will show you that there are many surprising possibilities for quilt designs that use only one kind of block. Learn to create even more block patterns using the exercises on page 82.

The eleven drawings for each block were designed to be used in various ways. The medium green area represents the primary block pattern, while the light gray area represents the secondary block pattern.

❖ Block pattern #1, #2, #6, or #9 can be used for repeat quilt designs.

❖ Block pattern #2 can be rotated to create unique repeat quilt designs or as the four-block center of a medallion.

❖ Block pattern #3, #4, or #5 can be used as one of the blocks in an alternate two-block design or as the center block of a medallion.

❖ Block pattern #6 or #9 can be used as one of the blocks in an alternate two-block design.

❖ Block pattern #7 can be used for borders in a medallion design or to create a strippy design.

❖ Block pattern #8 can be used around a center medallion block or to create a border corner in an on-point setting.

❖ Block pattern #10 can be used to border a center medallion, to create a quilt border, or for a strippy quilt design.

❖ Block pattern #11 can be used to turn corners in a medallion border design or to turn corners in quilt borders.

Aunt Vinah's Favorite

Hopscotch

Christmas Star

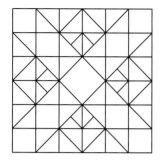

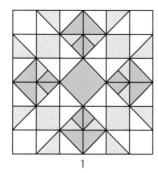
1

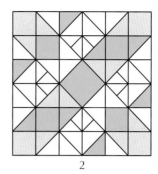
2

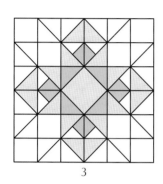
3

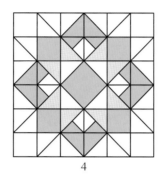
4

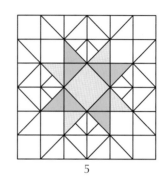
5

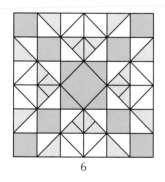
6

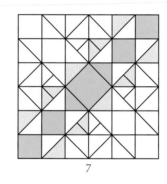
7

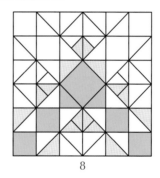
8

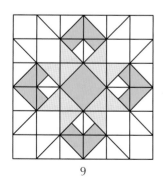
9

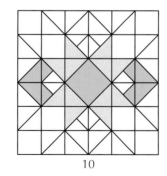
10

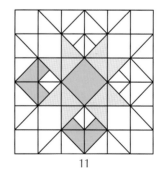
11

All Hallows

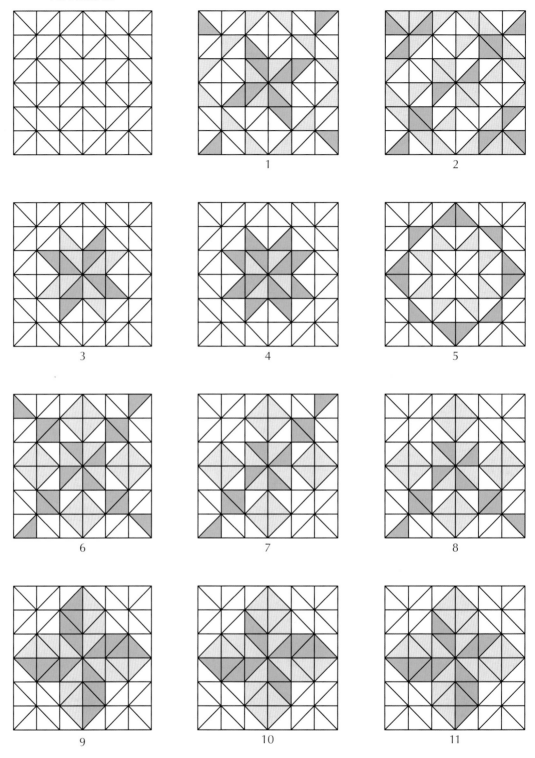

Capital T

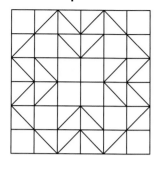

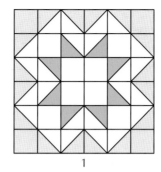

1

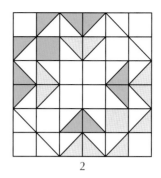

2

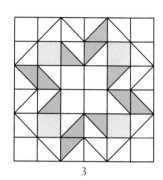

3

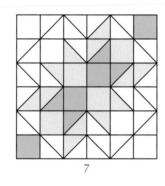

4

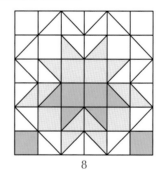

5

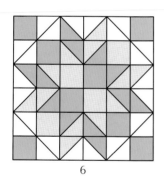

6

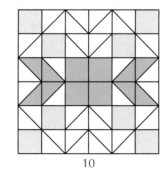

7

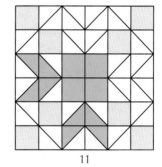

8

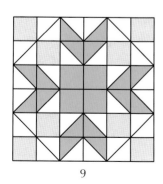

9

10

11

Wyoming Valley

Combination Star

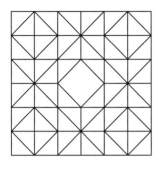

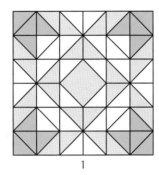

1

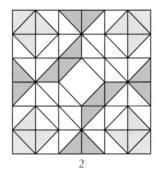

2

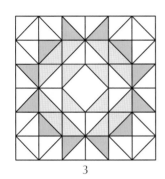

3

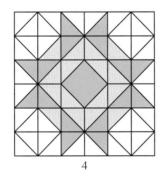

4

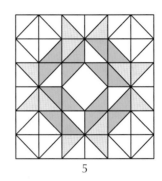

5

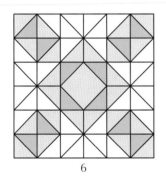

6

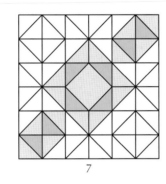

7

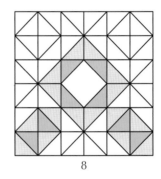

8

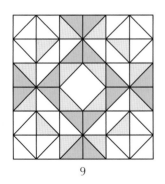

9

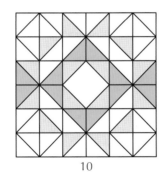

10

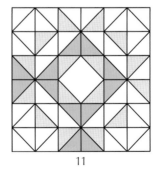

11

Swing in the Center

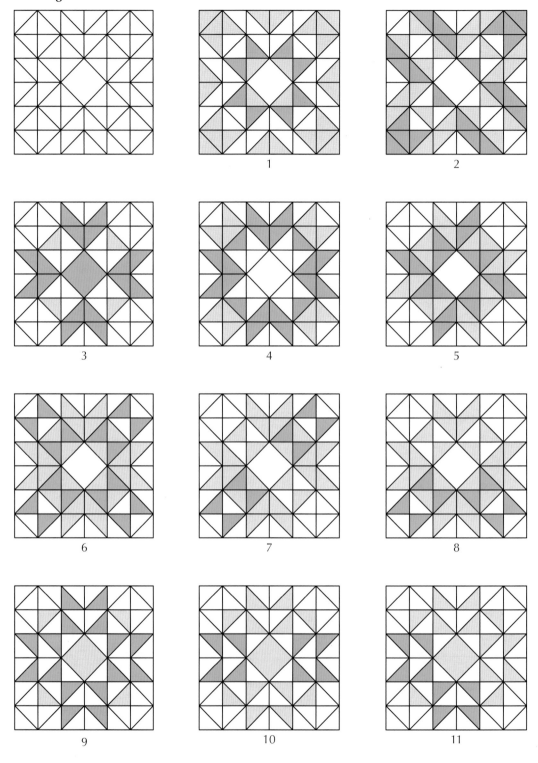

Jackknife

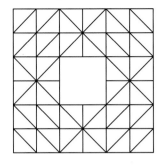

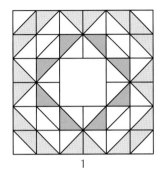

1

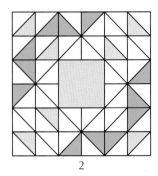

2

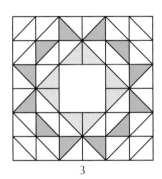

3

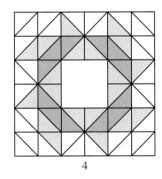

4

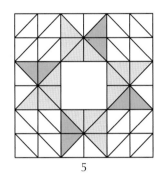

5

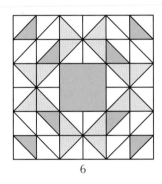

6

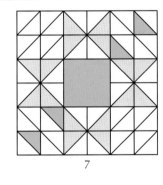

7

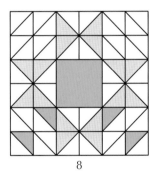

8

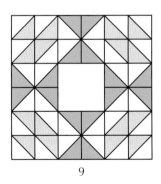

9

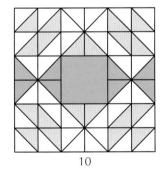

10

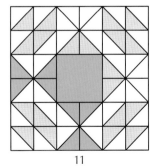

11

Courthouse Square

QUILT-DESIGN MOCK-UPS

Following are examples of each of the basic quilt designs, using some of the block patterns presented on the previous pages.

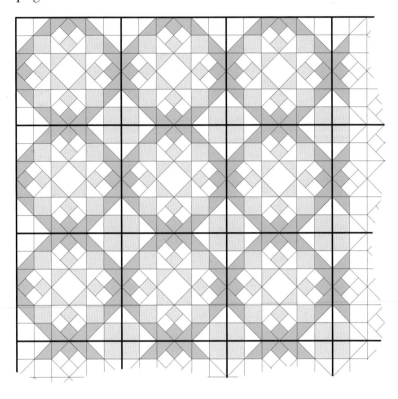

Repeat Block Design
Aunt Vinah's Favorite
Block Pattern #1
Note slight modification of block
to enhance border effect.

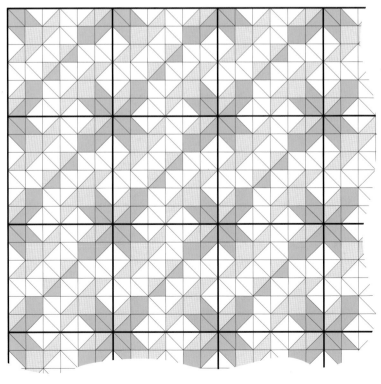

Repeat Block Design
Hopscotch
Block Pattern #2

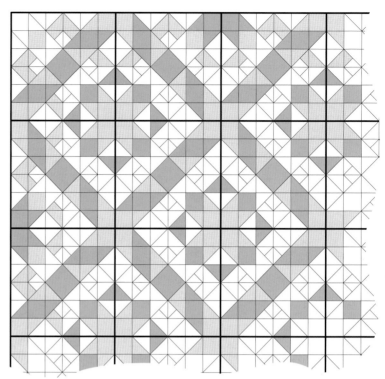

Repeat Block Design
Christmas Star
Block Pattern #2 rotated
Note modification of block for border effect.

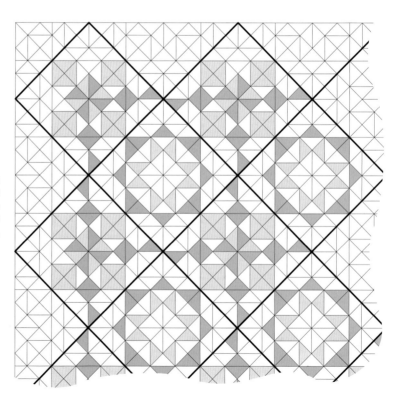

On-Point Alternate Block Design
All Hallows
Block Patterns #5, #6
Note use of Block Patterns #7 and #8
for border effect.

Alternate Block Design
Capital T
Block Patterns #5, #9
Note extension of Block Pattern #5 into border and
use of Block Patterns #10 and #11 for border effect.

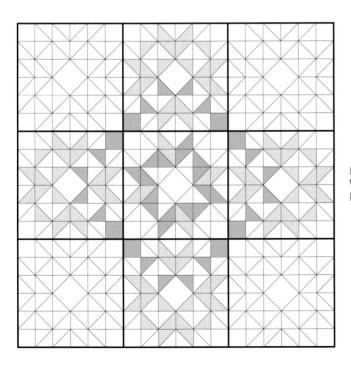

Medallion One-Block Center
Wyoming Valley
Blocks Patterns #5, #8

Medallion One-Block Center, On-Point
Combination Star
Block Patterns #3, #10, #11

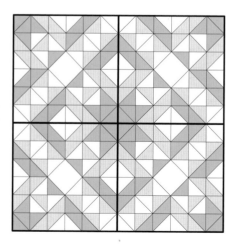

Medallion Four-Block Center
Swing in the Center
Block Pattern #2 rotated

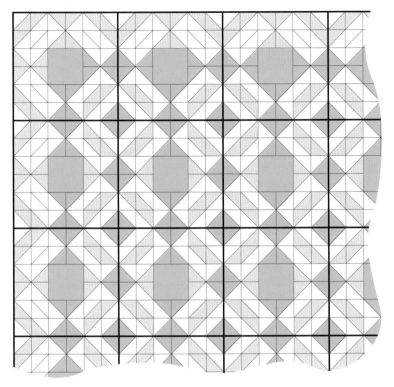

Strippy Quilt Design
Jackknife
Block Pattern #10
Note modification of block pattern on the sides
of the block to emphasize the strippy design
and at the outer edge of the quilt
and ends of rows to create a border effect.

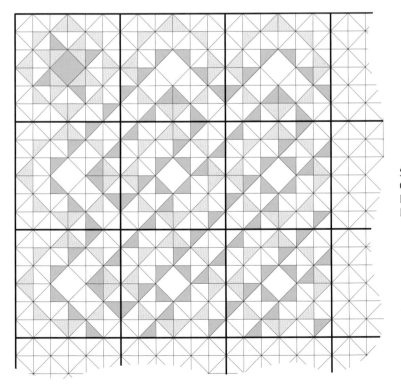

Strippy Quilt Design
Courthouse Square
Block Pattern #7
Note use of Block Pattern #8 for border effect.

BLOCK-PATTERN EXERCISES

Being creative is a matter of learning how to play. Definitions of play include "to move lightly, to amuse oneself, to participate in a game." Think of the following exercises, using your design board and your fabric, as games for your amusement. Take the process lightly. Many patterns happen by accident. Place your fabrics in crazy arrangements, remembering that you do not have to sew anything together. As you play, you will discover block patterns you may want to use in your next quilt design.

❖ Cover one or two fabrics on a completed block with a different fabric. Slight changes in fabric placement can have dramatic effects on block pattern.

❖ Reverse the placement of two fabrics within a block; for example, reverse the dark and focus fabric placements.

❖ Look for shapes such as boxes, stars, diamonds, or chevrons. Fill a shape with a single fabric color.

❖ Place fabric in areas at the sides or corners of the block first.

❖ Cover half of the block either vertically or diagonally and place fabrics in the remaining half; then repeat the pattern for the other half.

❖ Cover three-quarters of the block either vertically, horizontally, or diagonally and place fabric in the remaining quarter of the block; then repeat the pattern in the other three sections.

❖ Create a different block pattern in each half of the block either vertically, horizontally, or diagonally.

APPENDIX

FORMULA FOR DIAGONAL MEASUREMENTS

The following formula will give you an accurate diagonal measurement of any square block.

Multiply the length of the block side by 1.414.
Example: 12" x 12" block
12" x 1.414 = 16.968 → Round up to 17".

Block side x 1.414 = Diagonal

To find the measurement of the block *side* when you have the *diagonal* measurement, divide the length of the diagonal by 1.414.

Example: 17" diagonal
17" ÷ 1.414 = 12"

Diagonal ÷ 1.414 = Block side

SETTING TRIANGLES FOR ON-POINT SETTINGS

Cut 4 side setting triangles from a square as shown, so that the straight of grain runs along the long side of the triangles, which will be at the outside edge of the quilt. Cut 2 corner setting triangles from a square to keep the straight grain on the outer edges.

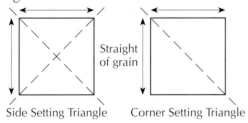

Side Setting Triangle   Corner Setting Triangle

Formula for Side Setting Triangles

To find the correct size to cut the squares for side setting triangles in on-point settings, use the following procedure.

Example: 12" x 12" block

1. Find the diagonal measurement of the block.
   Length of block side x 1.414 = Diagonal measurement
   12" x 1.414 = 16.968 → Round up to 17".

   17" is the *finished* length of the triangle side required to fit the quilt.

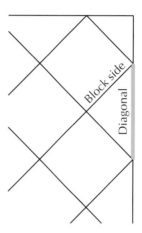

Block side x 1.414 = Diagonal

2. Add 1¼" to the diagonal measurement for the correct size to cut the square.
   17" + 1¼" = 18¼"

   Cut a square 18¼" x 18¼", then cut it twice diagonally for 4 side setting triangles.

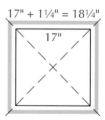

Diagonal + 1¼" = Block size to cut for triangles

Formula for Corner Setting Triangles

To find the correct size to cut the squares for corner setting triangles in on-point settings, use the following procedure.

Example: 12" x 12" block
1. The diagonal measurement of the corner block is 12", which is equal to the width of the blocks in the quilt. Find the finished length of the corner-block side.

   Diagonal measurement ÷ 1.414 = Corner-block side measurement

   12" ÷ 1.414 = 8.48" → Round up to 8.5".

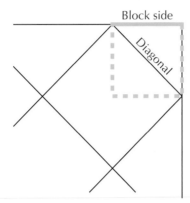

Diagonal ÷ 1.414 = Block side

2. Add ⅞" to find the cut size of the block.

   8½" + ⅞" = 9⅜"

   Cut a square 9⅜" x 9⅜", then cut it once diagonally for 2 corner setting triangles.

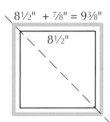

Block side measurement + ⅞" = Cut size of square

Magic Yardage Formula Card

This handy reference has been provided for your convenience. Copy the following, cut it out on the lines, and glue to opposite sides of a piece of card stock (or old business card). Laminate it, if you wish, and place it in your wallet as a quick guide for purchasing fabric.

Standard Mattress Sizes

Twin	38" x 75"
Full	53" x 75"
Queen	60" x 80"
King	76" x 80"

Water Beds

Super Single	48" x 84"
Queen	60" x 84"
King	72" x 84"

Add 15" to each side and end.

Add 15" to the length for pillow tuck.

Magic Yardage Formula

Width __" x Length __" ÷ 500 = Total Yards

Fabric Allotment:
Divide total yardage as follows:

½ = light	⅛ = medium
⅛ = focus	⅛ = accent
⅛ = dark	

Meet the Author

Raised in the fifties in a small, west-central Wisconsin community, Carole learned the basics of needle craft from her mother. For the next twenty years, she embroidered pillowcases, crocheted afghans, and knitted sweaters. Then, in 1974, Carole discovered quiltmaking. Over the next fifteen years, she made numerous award-winning quilts while trying a variety of quilting techniques, styles, and fabrics. It was over the last seven years that Carole discovered the technique of designing quilts through the use of block patterns.

Carole is enjoying the process of exploring her personal preferences through block pattern. "In following my personal hunches, I do not know where my journey will lead, but I do know that when I trust the process and let go of my fears, I discover amazing things," she says. To Carole, this journey is what makes quiltmaking so exciting.

Carole enjoys living in the country with her husband, John. Her children and grandchildren live nearby and are an important part of her life. When she is not quilting, you can find Carole researching and recording family history.

Carole is active in the Mixed Sampler Quilt Guild and Peacemakers Quilting Group. She teaches workshops and lectures on the block-pattern method of quilt design and continues to be amazed by the surprising designs her students create. For information on workshops and lectures and obtaining design boards, write to the author at 8163 Gorman Road, Danbury, Wisconsin 54830.

6.98